DIRT AND DESTRUCTION
SPORTS ZONE

TRACTOR PULLING
TEARING IT UP

BY PAUL HOBLIN

Lerner Publications Company • Minneapolis

Lerner Publications Company

A division of Lerner Publishing Group, Inc.

241 First Avenue North

Minneapolis, MN 55401 U.S.A.

For updated reading levels and more information, look up this title at www.lernerbooks.com.

Content Consultant: Charlene Bower, Bower Motorsports Media

Main body text set in Folio Std Light 11/17.
Typeface provided by Adobe Systems.

Library of Congress Cataloging-in-Publication Data
Hoblin, Paul.
    Tractor pulling : tearing it up / by Paul Hoblin.
      pages   cm. — (Dirt and destruction sports zone)
    Includes index.
    ISBN 978-1-4677-2123-3 (lib. bdg. : alk. paper)
    ISBN 978-1-4677-2455-5 (eBook)
    1. Tractor pulling (Motorsports) I. Title.
  TL233.3.H63 2014
  796.7—dc23   2013022637

Manufactured in the United States of America
1—VI—12-31-13

The images in this book are used with the permission of: © Alvey & Towers Picture Library/Alamy, pp. 4–5, 9; © Library of Congress, p. 6 (LC-USZ62-54516); © Margaret Bourke-White/Getty Images, p. 7; © Alfred Eisenstaedt/Getty Images, p. 8; © Steve Larson/The Denver Post/Getty Images, p. 10; © Keith Bell/Shutterstock Images, pp. 11, 12–13, 22; © imagebroker.net/SuperStock, p. 12 (top); © Dan Powers/Post-Crescent/AP Images, pp. 14–15; © picturesbyrob/Alamy, pp. 16, 19, 21; © imac/Alamy, p. 17; © Daniel Dempster Photography/Alamy, p. 18; © The Washington Post/Getty Images, p. 20; © ZUMA Press, Inc./Alamy, p. 23; © DaveDannPhotos.com, pp. 24, 25, 26, 27, 28, 29.

Front cover: © George Kroll/Dreamstime.com (main); © Janis Smits/Shutterstock.com (background).

TABLE OF CONTENTS

CHAPTER ONE

WHAT IS TRACTOR PULLING?

*T*ractor pulling is one of the most exciting motorsports events around. People all over the world flock to tractor-pulling competitions. Fans go to watch huge trucks and powerful tractors flex their muscles. These mighty machines pull incredible amounts of weight on a sled down a dirt track. The vehicle that can pull the most weight the farthest distance is the winner. Different competitions have different prizes. But the winning drivers usually take home prize money and a trophy.

During a tractor-pulling competition, drivers compete to see whose tractor is the most powerful.

STRONG HORSES

Pulling competitions have always been about power. But they weren't always about tractors. Steam-powered tractors were invented in the late 1860s. Then, in 1887, John Charter invented the first gasoline-fueled tractor in Illinois. But tractors didn't become common until many years later. Before tractors most farmers used horses to pull their plows. These horses needed to be very strong.

Sometimes farmers held competitions to see whose horse was the strongest. They usually started by removing a barn door.

HORSEPOWER

Horses are not often used to plow fields anymore. But horse pulling is still a popular sport. Horses are no match for modern-day tractors. But they are still plenty powerful. Just like any great athlete, the horses exercise daily to build up their pulling power. Their diet includes extra vitamins to help them pull big loads.

They laid the door flat on the ground. Then the farmers hitched the door to a horse. A farmer stood on the door. If the horse could pull both the door and the person, another farmer would be added. Then another. And another. Whichever horse pulled the most farmers the longest distance was the winner.

TRACTOR PULLING TAKES OFF

By the 1920s, many farmers had replaced horses with motorized tractors. Tractors are much more powerful than horses. Farmers wanted to test their tractors against one another. In 1929 the first known tractor-pulling competitions occurred in Vaughnsville, Ohio, and Bowling Green, Missouri.

A farmer gets his team of horses ready for a horse-pulling competition in 1950.

There were no official rules for these early tractor-pulling competitions. Instead of barn doors, the tractors dragged sleds. The sleds were loaded with people or other heavy objects. Sometimes a tractor would even drag another tractor! When the competitions were over, farmers took their tractors back to their fields. Their motto was "Pull on Sunday, plow on Monday."

As time went on, tractor pulling became popular at state and county fairs. Some people began modifying their tractors. This made the machines more powerful. They used the modified tractors only for competitions. Event organizers grouped competitions into different divisions. Each division included tractors that were most alike. The modified tractors no longer competed against regular field tractors. Some people began using strong pickup trucks to pull heavy loads.

Farmers needed their tractors to help with farmwork, so they brought their tractors back to the fields after competitions.

The tractors used at modern tractor-pulling competitions often look very different from those that were used during the sport's early days.

Other people used powerful vehicles called semitrucks to pull heavy trailers loaded with goods. These vehicles were added to events. Many people consider modern tractor pulling the world's most powerful motorsport.

Tractor pulling has changed a lot since the sport's early days. Drivers are finding new ways to pull heavier and heavier loads all the time. And the sport is more popular than ever. Fans love to hear engines roar as huge loads move down the track!

JUST PULL!

Some of the first-ever tractor pulls didn't take place on an official dirt track. Early tractor pullers picked an open space outside. Then they hooked a huge amount of weight to their tractors. The drivers tried to pull the weight 30 feet (9 meters). If they could do it, more weight was added. But tractors weren't as sturdy back then. The winner was often the tractor that made it 30 feet without falling apart.

TRACTOR-PULLING
RULES

W hen tractor pulling began in the late 1920s, different competitions had different rules. But everything changed in the late 1960s. In 1969 tractor pullers in eight US states—Illinois, Indiana, Iowa, Michigan, Minnesota, Missouri, Ohio, and Pennsylvania—got together. They formed the National Tractor Pullers

By the 1970s, tractor pulling was an official sport with standard rules.

If a tractor is able to pull the sled the full distance required, that driver has completed a full pull.

Association (NTPA). The NTPA created a set of rules that tractor-pulling competitions began to follow. This made tractor pulling an official sport.

GUIDELINES

The specific rules of tractor pulling still vary by competition. Different events have different rules about what types of tractors and trucks can be used. The length and the width of the track also varies. But most tracks are at least 30 feet (9 m) wide and 320 feet (97 m) long.

The trucks and the tractors are divided into groups called classes. The classes are based on weight, body, and engine type. No matter the class, all competitions have some things in common. The vehicles all attempt to pull a metal sled loaded with lots of weight for a certain distance. If a driver can do it, he or she has completed a full pull. Sometimes more than one driver makes a full pull. Then the successful drivers compete in a pull-off. More weight is added to each sled. Then each of the remaining tractors pulls the sled as far as possible. Whoever pulls the sled the farthest is the winner.

Tractor pulling is a popular sport in many European countries, including Germany.

In NTPA events, tractor pullers can earn points for each pull they attempt. These points are added up at the end of the season. The driver with the most points in each class is named the Grand National Champion for his or her class.

THE SLED

When tractor pulling first became a sport, the way to make a sled heavier was similar to horse pulls. People stood at designated spots along the track. They stepped onto the sled as the tractor passed them. The sled got heavier as the tractor moved forward.

Most tractor-pulling competitions now use a weight transfer sled.

TRACTOR PULLING GOES INTERNATIONAL

In 1977 Lester Houck and Mark Stauffer of the United States traveled to Holland and put on a tractor-pulling demonstration. The event was a huge success. Before long, tractor-pulling events were held around the world. Countries such as the United Kingdom, the Netherlands, Brazil, and Australia have tractor-pulling events. Each of these countries has its own ruling organization. But the basics of the sport are the same everywhere.

The step-on method needed to change as tractors became stronger. Pulling so much weight was hard on the tractors. Sometimes the engines caught on fire. Tractors rolled over. It wasn't safe for the people stepping onto the sled. The tractors had also become too powerful. People didn't weigh enough to slow them down.

Some competitions began using a deadweight sled. This meant the sled was loaded with all the weight before the tractor began to pull. Deadweight sleds were loaded with stones and concrete.

The weight transfer sled is the type of sled most modern competitions use. A weighted box sits on top of the weight transfer sled. Weighted blocks can be added to the box to make it heavier. The box moves from back to front along the sled as the tractor pulls it. As the box moves forward, the sled gets harder to pull.

BREAKDOWN OF A TRACTOR-PULL SLED

KILL SWITCH

The kill switch is mounted on a tractor's hitch. It is a small pin. When the pin is pulled out, the tractor immediately turns off. The sled operator can trigger the kill switch from the sled. Doing so immediately stops the tractor.

HOOK

The hook connects the tractor to the sled.

BOX

A box travels from the back of the sled to the front as the tractor moves forward. The weighted box can weigh up to 65,000 pounds (29,500 kilograms). Weighted blocks can be added to the box to make it heavier.

SLED OPERATOR

A person sits at the end of each tractor or truck's weight transfer sled. This person is known as the sled operator. The sled operator's job is to make sure the tractor remains in control as it tries to pull the sled. If something goes wrong, the sled operator triggers a kill switch.

PAN

As the box moves forward on the sled, it puts more force on a pan that is built onto the bottom of the sled. This forces the pan down until it touches the track. The more weight that goes forward, the more the pan touches the track. This causes increasing amounts of friction. Eventually the friction will be enough to stop the tractor.

15

This tractor's engine caught fire at a tractor pull in Denmark.

SAFETY RULES

Weight transfer sleds made for better and safer competitions. But accidents still happened. Tractors kept getting more powerful. The sport needed more safety rules. In 1971 the NTPA came up with stricter vehicle requirements. Kill switches and other safety features were added to

THE LEVELS OF TRACTOR PULLING

NTPA competitions take place on four different levels. The state level is the lowest NTPA level. This is where most rookie tractor pullers get their starts. The next level up is the regional level. Regional competitors are often as skilled as higher-level drivers. However, there are fewer regional competitions. Many pullers choose to compete at this level because it takes up less of their time. The Grand National level has some of the best competitors and equipment in the sport. Grand National competitions take place across the country. The final level is the super national level. The super national level consists of the top Grand National events. The competitors at the super national and Grand National levels are usually the same. But super national competitions usually have bigger prizes than Grand National competitions.

tractors and sleds. These parts are designed to keep everyone safe. Drivers whose tractors don't meet these requirements are disqualified. Safety is the most important thing in tractor pulling.

All professional tractor drivers are required to wear helmets. They also wear fireproof suits. Concrete barriers protect spectators from engine fires. Before every event, officials examine each tractor carefully. They make sure all the parts of the tractor are working as they should.

Most tractors and trucks used in tractor pulls use engines that burn diesel fuel. The diesel-powered tractors give off black smoke as they pull their heavy loads. The smoke creates another safety hazard at tractor pulls. This is especially true at indoor arenas. The smoke is bad for everyone's health. For everyone's safety, sleds are attached to smoke machines at indoor events. The machines suck up the exhaust and send it out of the arena.

TRACTORS
AND TRUCKS

As the sport of tractor pulling evolved, the tractors themselves underwent huge changes. One change was made by Noble Harrison of Pittsfield, Illinois, in 1972. He used an engine with a two-stage turbocharging system. Turbochargers increase engine power. But the new turbochargers made engines very hot. The engines became so hot they could melt. Water-injection systems were added to cool these engines down.

MANY ENGINES

While some drivers were trying to increase an engine's power, others were trying to increase the number of engines in a tractor.

Modern tractors are more powerful than ever before.

In 1973 two brothers from Ohio put together the first cross box. The cross box was a device that allowed Carl and Paul Bosse to link two engines together on one tractor. Other drivers soon began using and improving upon the Bosses' invention.

In the 1970s, brothers Ralph and Dave Banter drove the first tractor with three engines. In 1980 the brothers added a fourth engine. Then another. And another. By the late 1980s, the Banters drove two tractors. The tractors were known as *Mr. Chevy* and *Bandit*. Each one had six engines. Rather than try to fit the engines into the tractor, the Banter brothers fit the tractor around the engines. They first laid out the engines. Then they built the tractor around them. However, the tractor parts couldn't handle that much power. Multiple engines quickly destroy tractors' transmissions and clutches. As a result, a slipper clutch, also called a slider, was invented. This clutch worked automatically. The driver didn't need to push the clutch pedal to put the tractor in gear. This type of clutch put less stress on the transmission.

Along with engine changes, there were also dramatic increases in wheel speeds. Modern tractor wheels can spin over 100 miles (160 kilometers) per hour. Tractors never actually move anywhere near that fast because of the heavy sled. But the increased wheel speed allows tractors to pull more weight than ever before.

Drivers also began increasing tire size. Bigger tires help support the tractor's weight. They also provide traction. The more weight a tractor is trying to pull, the bigger the back tires it needs. The front tires steer and support the weight of the front of the tractor.

THE CLASSES

There are many different types of competitive tractors and trucks. Truck classes range from four-wheel-drive pickup trucks to huge semitrucks. Tractor classes range from small garden tractors to huge field tractors. The classes are divided into two main categories, stock and modified.

Stock tractors must look like regular field tractors from the outside. But their engines have much more power. The engines are typically fitted with turbochargers to increase their horsepower. Stock tractors typically come with diesel engines. But drivers

Many tractor pulls also feature pickup trucks pulling heavy loads.

Some mini tractors are modified to look nothing like regular garden tractors.

may modify their tractors to burn alcohol fuel. Diesel engines usually burn more efficiently. Alcohol engines typically burn cleaner.

Modified tractors are even more powerful than stock tractors. These vehicles don't look much like tractors you may see in a field. Usually the body panels have been removed. Modified tractors can have many engines. The tractors may also have larger back tires than stock tractors.

COMPETITIVE CRUISERS

Not all tractors are big and powerful. Another type of pulling tractor is the mini. The mini is a modified garden tractor. This is the type of machine someone might use to mow a lawn. Many competitions also have an antique division. These old tractors are restored and modified for greater pulling ability.

There may be no natural limit to how many engines a tractor can hold. To make the competitions fair, the NTPA and other tractor-pulling organizations set their own limits. A tractor can only compete in a certain division if it meets certain requirements.

Many different divisions exist within the stock and modified classes. The NTPA Grand National level has 11 different divisions. These divisions include super farm, super stock, pro stock, unlimited, super semi, and more. The NTPA regional and state levels have even more divisions.

The type of pulling vehicle, the vehicle's weight, tire size, and other engine-related restrictions determine these divisions. For example, super farm tractors closely resemble field tractors. Super farm engines can only have one turbocharger. They must run on diesel fuel and meet a 9,300-pound (4,200 kg) weight limit. Pro stock engines can have four turbochargers. Unlimited

Stock tractors look like regular tractors that might be seen working in a farmer's field.

Modified tractors can look very different from typical field tractors.

has the fewest restrictions. The tractors must meet safety restrictions and the 8,000-pound (3,600 kg) weight limit. Any other changes are allowed. The semitruck divisions have the heaviest vehicles. In super semi, the truck must look like a regular semitruck. It also must meet a 20,000-pound (9,072 kg) weight limit.

Competitive tractors are specialized vehicles. Some of them still look like field tractors on the outside. But others would be unrecognizable to most farmers.

AMAZING ENGINES

The unlimited modified division is known for its powerful engines. Many engines come from other powerful vehicles, such as jets, torpedo boats, and tanks. A single unlimited modified tractor may have as many as five jet engines powering it. These engines may have as much as 4,000 horsepower per engine.

CHAPTER FOUR

THE DRIVERS

Tractor-pulling drivers are skilled and creative. Thanks to them and their amazing vehicles, tractor pulling has become a popular sport around the world. Drivers continue to push the limits of tractor pulling. In fact, there are more drivers and tractor classes than ever before.

Adam Koester drives a mini tractor sponsored by Shell. Sponsors help financially support tractor pullers.

A DRIVER'S LIFE

Tractor pulling can be an expensive sport. It costs a lot of money to turn a regular truck or tractor into a powerful pulling machine. Many drivers who compete at the national

level have sponsors. The sponsors help support the driver with money. In return, the drivers advertise for their sponsors. Most tractor pullers are also part of a team. A team usually consists of the driver and a few mechanics. The team works together to make sure the tractor is ready to pull a huge load. Many teams consist of drivers and their family members.

KEN VENEY

Ken Veney was a legend in motorsports long before he began driving tractors. Veney got his start racing hot rods in the 1960s. These are cars that have been modified to be extra fast. In 2000 Veney made the switch to tractor pulling. In 2012 he drove his tractor, *Funny Farmall*, in the unlimited modified class.

That year Veney won the first NTPA Grand National event of 2012 in Tomah, Wisconsin. The next several competitions also went well for Veney. But then he discovered his tractor's rear end was damaged. Another competition was scheduled to take place the next day. If the team couldn't find a way to fix the tractor, Veney wouldn't be able to pull. He also could miss several events in the weeks ahead. But Veney and his crew stayed up all night. They managed to fix the tractor's rear end so Veney could compete.

At the end of the season, Veney was the overall points leader. This made him the 2012 Grand National Unlimited Modified Champion.

In addition to driving, Ken Veney also designs and builds parts for tractor pulling.

Adam Bauer drives a super stock tractor at a 2013 NTPA Grand National event in Hutchinson, Minnesota.

ADAM BAUER

In 2012 a new division called the light unlimited division was introduced. Light unlimited division tractors must weigh less than 6,000 pounds (2,700 kg). But they have few other restrictions. Many drivers build tractors to compete in this class. But Adam Bauer stands out from the pack. He won the first NTPA Grand National event in Tomah, Wisconsin, by more than 30 feet (9 m). His next pull took place in Arcola, Indiana. He experienced some mechanical problems. But he still managed to finish seventh.

The event in Arcola was the only time Bauer didn't place first in 2012. He finished the season with the most points. This meant he was the NTPA's Grand National Champion in the light unlimited class. It was his fourth championship in three different classes. He had earned two mini titles and one modified title in past seasons.

Bret Berg was the Grand National Modified Champion in 2011 and 2012.

BRET BERG

Veteran puller Bret Berg has been competing for more than 30 years. In 2012 Berg competed in the modified class. He had won the Grand National Championship in the modified class in 2011. Berg's fans hoped he could do it again. Berg damaged his tractor, *Money Maker*, in the first NTPA Grand National event. But he made repairs and managed a second-place finish in the next competition. Berg took first place in the season's third event. By then there were three tractors that stood a chance to win the points race: Berg's *Money Maker*, Jim Martell's *Wild Won*, and rookie Brad Benedict's *Non Cent$*. In the end, Berg came out on top by racking up six first-place finishes.

GEORGE TOONE

One of the great things about tractor pulling is that anyone with courage and the right skills can do it. George Toone competes in the antique tractor class. Toone has been blind his whole life. But that hasn't stopped him from fixing up and driving his competitive tractors.

Jerry Walker was the NTPA's 2012 Grand National Champion in the super semi class.

Toone operates the vehicle. His wife, Amy, offers instructions and directions through a radio. Sometimes she'll hop aboard with him.

MILESTONE MOMENTS

In 1978 Julie Sporhase became the first female driver to qualify for the Indy Super Pull. This is one of the biggest competitions in tractor pulling. Sporhase paved the way for many other female drivers. In 1991 Rodalyn Knox was the first woman to win an Indy Super Pull title. She competed in the unlimited modified class. That year she also finished third in the Grand National points standings. Male drivers once dominated tractor pulling. But the sport is open to any driver who has the skill and a tractor or a truck able to pull huge amounts of weight.

Becoming a tractor-pulling driver takes a lot of skill and a lot of time. But all drivers start somewhere. Check out a competition at your county or state fair to learn more about tractor pulling. You can also attend one of the many NTPA events held each year. These events take place throughout the country.

Someday you may be able to modify and drive a tractor of your own!

GLOSSARY

CLUTCH

a mechanical device that connects and disconnects with a vehicle's transmission

CROSS BOX

an invention that made it possible to link multiple engines

FRICTION

the rubbing of one object against another

FULL PULL

when a tractor pulls a sled the length of the track

HORSEPOWER

the unit that measures engine power in the United States

MOTTO

a short saying that expresses a belief

SLED OPERATOR

the person in charge of working the sled and kill switch

SPONSOR

a company that financially supports an individual so he or she can focus on an activity

TRANSMISSION

a mechanical device that moves power from a vehicle's engine to its wheels

FOR MORE INFORMATION

FURTHER READING

Abramson, Andrea Serlin. *Heavy Equipment Up Close*. New York: Sterling, 2007.

Sutcliffe, Jane. *John Deere*. Minneapolis: Lerner Publications Company, 2007.

Waxman, Laura Hamilton. *Terrific Transportation Inventions*. Minneapolis: Lerner
    Publications Company, 2014.

WEBSITES

National Tractor Pulling Association
http://www.ntpapull.com/
The official website of the NTPA features information about tractor pulling,
including videos, rules, and upcoming events.

PullingReference.com
http://www.pulling-reference.com/
This website features statistics from tractor-pulling competitions dating back to
the 1970s.

Tractor Pulling
http://www.livinghistoryfarm.org/farminginthe50s/machines_09.html
Visit this website to learn more about the history of tractors and tractor pulling.

INDEX

ABOUT THE AUTHOR

Paul Hoblin has a master of fine arts degree from the University of Minnesota. He lives in Saint Paul, Minnesota.